FOREWORD

The collection of "Everything Will Be Okay" travel phrasebooks published by T&P Books is designed for people traveling abroad for tourism and business. The phrasebooks contain what matters most - the essentials for basic communication. This is an indispensable set of phrases to "survive" while abroad.

This phrasebook will help you in most cases where you need to ask something, get directions, find out how much something costs, etc. It can also resolve difficult communication situations where gestures just won't help.

This book contains a lot of phrases that have been grouped according to the most relevant topics. You'll also find a mini dictionary with useful words - numbers, time, calendar, colors...

Take "Everything Will Be Okay" phrasebook with you on the road and you'll have an irreplaceable traveling companion who will help you find your way out of any situation and teach you to not fear speaking with foreigners.

TABLE OF CONTENTS

T&P Books Publishing

T&P Books Publishing

PHRASEBOOK

— CZECH —

THE MOST IMPORTANT PHRASES

This phrasebook contains
the most important
phrases and questions
for basic communication
Everything you need
to survive overseas

By Andrey Taranov

T&P BOOKS

Phrasebook + 250-word dictionary

English-Czech phrasebook & mini dictionary

By Andrey Taranov

The collection of "Everything Will Be Okay" travel phrasebooks published by T&P Books is designed for people traveling abroad for tourism and business. The phrasebooks contain what matters most - the essentials for basic communication. This is an indispensable set of phrases to "survive" while abroad.

You'll also find a mini dictionary with 250 useful words required for everyday communication - the names of months and days of the week, measurements, family members, and more.

T&P Books Publishing
www.tpbooks.com

ISBN: 978-1-78492-414-0

This book is also available in E-book formats.
Please visit www.tpbooks.com or the major online bookstores.

PRONUNCIATION

T&P phonetic alphabet	Czech example	English example
[a]	lavina [lavɪna]	shorter than in ask
[aː]	banán [banaːn]	calf, palm
[e]	beseda [bɛsɛda]	elm, medal
[ɛː]	chléb [xlɛːp]	longer than bed, fell
[ɪ]	Bible [bɪblɛ]	big, America
[iː]	chudý [xudiː]	feet, meter
[o]	epocha [ɛpoxa]	pod, John
[oː]	diagnóza [dɪagnoːza]	fall, bomb
[u]	dokument [dokumɛnt]	book
[uː]	chůva [xuːva]	pool, room
[b]	babička [babɪtʃka]	baby, book
[ts]	celnice [tsɛlnɪtsɛ]	cats, tsetse fly
[tʃ]	vlčák [vltʃaːk]	church, French
[x]	archeologie [arxɛologɪe]	as in Scots 'loch'
[d]	delfín [dɛlfiːn]	day, doctor
[dʲ]	Holanďan [holandʲan]	median, radio
[f]	atmosféra [atmosfɛːra]	face, food
[g]	galaxie [galaksɪe]	game, gold
[h]	knihovna [knɪhovna]	huge, hat
[j]	jídlo [jiːdlo]	yes, New York
[k]	zaplakat [zaplakat]	clock, kiss
[l]	chlapec [xlapɛts]	lace, people
[m]	modelář [modɛlaːrʃ]	magic, milk
[n]	imunita [ɪmunɪta]	name, normal
[nʲ]	báseň [baːsɛnʲ]	canyon, new
[ŋk]	vstupenka [vstupɛŋka]	bank, trunk
[p]	poločas [polotʃas]	pencil, private
[r]	senátor [sɛnaːtor]	rice, radio
[rʒ], [rʃ]	bouřka [bourʃka]	urgent, flash
[s]	svoboda [svoboda]	city, boss
[ʃ]	šiška [ʃɪʃka]	machine, shark
[t]	turista [turɪsta]	tourist, trip
[tʲ]	poušť [pouʃtʲ]	tune, student
[v]	veverka [vɛvɛrka]	very, river
[z]	zapomínat [zapomiːnat]	zebra, please
[ʒ]	ložisko [loʒɪsko]	forge, pleasure

LIST OF ABBREVIATIONS

English abbreviations

ab.	-	about
adj	-	adjective
adv	-	adverb
anim.	-	animate
as adj	-	attributive noun used as adjective
e.g.	-	for example
etc.	-	et cetera
fam.	-	familiar
fem.	-	feminine
form.	-	formal
inanim.	-	inanimate
masc.	-	masculine
math	-	mathematics
mil.	-	military
n	-	noun
pl	-	plural
pron.	-	pronoun
sb	-	somebody
sing.	-	singular
sth	-	something
v aux	-	auxiliary verb
vi	-	intransitive verb
vi, vt	-	intransitive, transitive verb
vt	-	transitive verb

Czech abbreviations

ž	-	feminine noun
ž mn	-	feminine plural
m	-	masculine noun
m mn	-	masculine plural
m, ž	-	masculine, feminine
mn	-	plural
s	-	neuter
s mn	-	neuter plural

T&P BOOKS

CZECH
PHRASEBOOK

This section contains
important phrases that may
come in handy in various
real-life situations.
The phrasebook will help
you ask for directions, clarify
a price, buy tickets, and
order food at a restaurant

T&P Books Publishing

PHRASEBOOK CONTENTS

T&P Books Publishing

The bare minimum

Excuse me, ...	**Promiňte, ...** [promɪnʲtɛ, ...]
Hello.	**Dobrý den.** [dobri: dɛn]
Thank you.	**Děkuji.** [dekujɪ]
Good bye.	**Na shledanou.** [na sxlɛdanou]
Yes.	**Ano.** [ano]
No.	**Ne.** [nɛ]
I don't know.	**Nevím.** [nɛvi:m]
Where? | Where to? | When?	**Kde? | Kam? | Kdy?** [gdɛ? | kam? | gdɪ?]

I need ...	**Potřebuju ...** [potrʒebuju ...]
I want ...	**Chci ...** [xtsɪ ...]
Do you have ...?	**Máte ...?** [ma:tɛ ...?]
Is there a ... here?	**Je tady ...?** [jɛ tadɪ ...?]
May I ...?	**Můžu ...?** [mu:ʒu ...?]
..., please (polite request)	**..., prosím** [..., prosi:m]

I'm looking for ...	**Hledám ...** [hlɛda:m ...]
the restroom	**toaletu** [toalɛtu]
an ATM	**bankomat** [baŋkomat]
a pharmacy (drugstore)	**lékárnu** [lɛ:ka:rnu]
a hospital	**nemocnici** [nɛmotsnɪtsɪ]
the police station	**policejní stanici** [polɪtsɛjni: stanɪtsɪ]
the subway	**metro** [mɛtro]

a taxi	**taxík** [taksi:k]
the train station	**vlakové nádraží** [vlakovɛ: na:draʒi:]

My name is …	**Jmenuju se …** [jmɛnuju sɛ …]
What's your name?	**Jak se jmenujete?** [jak sɛ jmɛnujɛtɛ?]
Could you please help me?	**Můžete mi prosím pomoct?** [mu:ʒetɛ mɪ prosi:m pomotst?]
I've got a problem.	**Mám problém.** [ma:m problɛ:m]
I don't feel well.	**Necítím se dobře.** [nɛtsi:ti:m sɛ dobrʒɛ]
Call an ambulance!	**Zavolejte sanitku!** [zavolɛjtɛ sanɪtku!]
May I make a call?	**Můžu si zavolat?** [mu:ʒu sɪ zavolat?]

I'm sorry.	**Omlouvám se.** [omlouva:m sɛ]
You're welcome.	**Není zač.** [nɛni: zatʃ]

I, me	**Já** [ja:]
you (inform.)	**ty** [tɪ]
he	**on** [on]
she	**ona** [ona]
they (masc.)	**oni** [onɪ]
they (fem.)	**ony** [onɪ]
we	**my** [mɪ]
you (pl)	**vy** [vɪ]
you (sg, form.)	**vy** [vɪ]

ENTRANCE	**VCHOD** [vxot]
EXIT	**VÝCHOD** [vi:xot]
OUT OF ORDER	**MIMO PROVOZ** [mɪmo provos]
CLOSED	**ZAVŘENO** [zavrʒɛno]

OPEN	**OTEVŘENO**
	[otɛvrʒɛno]
FOR WOMEN	**ŽENY**
	[ʒenɪ]
FOR MEN	**MUŽI**
	[muʒɪ]

Questions

Where?	**Kde?** [gdɛ?]
Where to?	**Kam?** [kam?]
Where from?	**Odkud?** [otkut?]
Why?	**Proč?** [protʃ?]
For what reason?	**Z jakého důvodu?** [z jakɛːho duːvodu?]
When?	**Kde?** [gdɛ?]

How long?	**Jak dlouho?** [jak dlouho?]
At what time?	**V kolik hodin?** [v kolɪk hodɪn?]
How much?	**Kolik?** [kolɪk?]
Do you have ...?	**Máte ...?** [maːtɛ ...?]
Where is ...?	**Kde je ...?** [gdɛ jɛ ...?]

What time is it?	**Kolik je hodin?** [kolɪk jɛ hodɪn?]
May I make a call?	**Můžu si zavolat?** [muːʒu sɪ zavolat?]
Who's there?	**Kdo je tam?** [gdo jɛ tam?]
Can I smoke here?	**Můžu tady kouřit?** [muːʒu tadɪ kourʒɪt?]
May I ...?	**Můžu ...?** [muːʒu ...?]

Needs

I'd like …	**Rád /Ráda/ bych …** [raːd /raːda/ bɪx …]
I don't want …	**Nechci …** [nɛxtsɪ …]
I'm thirsty.	**Mám žízeň.** [maːm ʒiːzɛnʲ]
I want to sleep.	**Chce se mi spát.** [xtsɛ sɛ mɪ spaːt]

I want …	**Chci …** [xtsɪ …]
to wash up	**se umýt** [sɛ umiːt]
to brush my teeth	**si vyčistit zuby** [sɪ vɪtʃɪstɪt zubɪ]
to rest a while	**si chvilku odpočinout** [sɪ xvɪlku otpotʃɪnout]
to change my clothes	**se převléknout** [sɛ prʒɛvlɛːknout]

to go back to the hotel	**se vrátit do hotelu** [sɛ vraːtɪt do hotɛlu]
to buy …	**si koupit …** [sɪ koupɪt …]
to go to …	**jít do …** [jiːt do …]
to visit …	**navštívit …** [navʃtiːvɪt …]
to meet with …	**se setkat s …** [sɛ sɛtkat s …]
to make a call	**si zavolat** [sɪ zavolat]

I'm tired.	**Jsem unavený /unavená/.** [jsɛm unavɛniː /unavɛnaː/]
We are tired.	**Jsme unavení /unaveny/.** [jsmɛ unavɛniː /unavɛnɪ/]
I'm cold.	**Je mi zima.** [jɛ mɪ zɪma]
I'm hot.	**Je mi horko.** [jɛ mɪ horko]
I'm OK.	**Jsem v pořádku.** [jsɛm v porʒaːtku]

I need to make a call.

Potřebuju si zavolat.
[potrʒɛbuju sɪ zavolat]

I need to go to the restroom.

Potřebuju jít na toaletu.
[potrʒɛbuju jiːt na toalɛtu]

I have to go.

Musím už jít.
[musiːm uʒ jiːt]

I have to go now.

Teď už musím jít.
[tɛtʲ uʒ musiːm jiːt]

Asking for directions

Excuse me, ...	**Promiňte, ...** [promɪnˈtɛ, ...]
Where is ...?	**Kde je ...?** [gdɛ jɛ ...?]
Which way is ...?	**Kudy ...?** [kudɪ ...?]
Could you help me, please?	**Můžete mi prosím pomoct?** [muːʒetɛ mɪ prosiːm pomotst?]
I'm looking for ...	**Hledám ...** [hlɛdaːm ...]
I'm looking for the exit.	**Hledám východ.** [hlɛdaːm viːxot]
I'm going to ...	**Jdu ...** [jdu ...]
Am I going the right way to ...?	**Jdu správným směrem do ...?** [jdu spraːvniːm smnɛrɛm do ...?]
Is it far?	**Je to daleko?** [jɛ to dalɛko?]
Can I get there on foot?	**Dostanu se tam pěšky?** [dostanu sɛ tam peʃkɪ?]
Can you show me on the map?	**Můžete mi to ukázat na mapě?** [muːʒetɛ mɪ to ukaːzat na mapɛ?]
Show me where we are right now.	**Ukažte mi, kde právě teď jsme.** [ukaʃtɛ mɪ, gdɛ praːve tɛdʲ jsmɛ]
Here	**Tady** [tadɪ]
There	**Tam** [tam]
This way	**Tudy** [tudɪ]
Turn right.	**Odbočte doprava.** [odbotʃtɛ doprava]
Turn left.	**Odbočte doleva.** [odbotʃtɛ dolɛva]
first (second, third) turn	**první (druhá, třetí) odbočka** [prvni: (druha:, trʒɛti:) odbotʃka]
to the right	**doprava** [doprava]

to the left

doleva
[dolɛva]

Go straight ahead.

Jděte stále rovně.
[jdetɛ staːlɛ rovne]

Signs

WELCOME!	**VÍTEJTE!** [vi:tɛjtɛ!]
ENTRANCE	**VCHOD** [vxot]
EXIT	**VÝCHOD** [vi:xot]

PUSH	**TLAČIT** [tlatʃɪt]
PULL	**TÁHNOUT** [ta:hnout]
OPEN	**OTEVŘENO** [otɛvrʒɛno]
CLOSED	**ZAVŘENO** [zavrʒɛno]

FOR WOMEN	**ŽENY** [ʒenɪ]
FOR MEN	**MUŽI** [muʒɪ]
GENTLEMEN, GENTS	**PÁNI** [pa:nɪ]
WOMEN	**DÁMY** [da:mɪ]

DISCOUNTS	**VÝPRODEJ** [vi:prodɛj]
SALE	**VÝPRODEJ** [vi:prodɛj]
FREE	**ZDARMA** [zdarma]
NEW!	**NOVINKA!** [novɪŋka!]
ATTENTION!	**POZOR!** [pozor!]

NO VACANCIES	**PLNĚ OBSAZENO** [plne opsazɛno]
RESERVED	**REZERVACE** [rɛzɛrvatsɛ]
ADMINISTRATION	**VEDENÍ** [vɛdɛni:]
STAFF ONLY	**VSTUP JEN PRO ZAMĚSTNANCE** [vstup jɛn pro zamnestnantsɛ]

BEWARE OF THE DOG! **POZOR PES!**
[pozor pɛs!]

NO SMOKING! **ZÁKAZ KOUŘENÍ**
[zaːkaz kourʒɛniː]

DO NOT TOUCH! **NEDOTÝKEJTE SE**
[nɛdotiːkɛjtɛ sɛ]

DANGEROUS **ŽIVOTU NEBEZPEČNÉ**
[ʒɪvotu nɛbɛzpɛtʃnɛː]

DANGER **NEBEZPEČNÉ**
[nɛbɛspɛtʃnɛː]

HIGH VOLTAGE **VYSOKÉ NAPĚTÍ**
[vɪsokɛː napetiː]

NO SWIMMING! **ZÁKAZ KOUPÁNÍ**
[zaːkaz koupaːniː]

OUT OF ORDER **MIMO PROVOZ**
[mɪmo provos]

FLAMMABLE **HOŘLAVÉ**
[horʒlavɛː]

FORBIDDEN **ZAKÁZÁNO**
[zakaːzaːno]

NO TRESPASSING! **ZÁKAZ VSTUPU**
[zaːkaz vstupu]

WET PAINT **ČERSTVĚ NATŘENO**
[tʃerstve natrʃeno]

CLOSED FOR RENOVATIONS **UZAVŘENO Z DŮVODU REKONSTRUKCE**
[uzavrʒeno z duːvodu rɛkonstruktsɛ]

WORKS AHEAD **PRÁCE NA SILNICI**
[praːtsɛ na sɪlnɪtsɪ]

DETOUR **OBJÍŽĎKA**
[objiːʒtʲka]

Transportation. General phrases

plane	**letadlo** [lɛtadlo]
train	**vlak** [vlak]
bus	**autobus** [autobus]
ferry	**trajekt** [trajɛkt]
taxi	**taxík** [taksi:k]
car	**auto** [auto]
schedule	**jízdní řád** [ji:zdni: rʒa:t]
Where can I see the schedule?	**Kde se můžu podívat na jízdní řád?** [gdɛ sɛ mu:ʒu podi:vat na ji:zdni: rʒa:t?]
workdays (weekdays)	**pracovní dny** [pratsovni: dnɪ]
weekends	**víkendy** [vi:kɛndɪ]
holidays	**prázdniny** [pra:zdnɪnɪ]
DEPARTURE	**ODJEZD** [odjɛst]
ARRIVAL	**PŘÍJEZD** [prʃi:jɛst]
DELAYED	**ZPOŽDĚNÍ** [zpoʒdeni:]
CANCELLED	**ZRUŠENO** [zruʃeno]
next (train, etc.)	**příští** [prʃi:ʃti:]
first	**první** [prvni:]
last	**poslední** [poslɛdni:]
When is the next ...?	**Kdy jede příští ...?** [gdɪ jɛdɛ prʒi:ʃti: ...?]
When is the first ...?	**Kdy jede první ...?** [gdɪ jɛdɛ prvni: ...?]

When is the last ...?

Kdy jede poslední ...?
[gdɪ jɛdɛ poslɛdni: ...?]

transfer (change of trains, etc.)

přestup
[prʃɛstup]

to make a transfer

přestoupit
[prʃɛstoupɪt]

Do I need to make a transfer?

Musím přestupovat?
[musi:m prʃɛstupovat?]

Buying tickets

Where can I buy tickets?	**Kde si mohu koupit jízdenky?** [gdɛ sɪ mohu koupɪt ji:zdɛŋkɪ?]
ticket	**jízdenka** [ji:zdɛŋka]
to buy a ticket	**koupit si jízdenku** [koupɪt sɪ ji:zdɛŋku]
ticket price	**cena jízdenky** [tsɛna ji:zdɛŋkɪ]
Where to?	**Kam?** [kam?]
To what station?	**Do jaké stanice?** [do jakɛ: stanɪtsɛ?]
I need …	**Potřebuju …** [potrʒɛbuju …]
one ticket	**jednu jízdenku** [jɛdnu ji:zdɛŋku]
two tickets	**dvě jízdenky** [dve ji:zdɛŋkɪ]
three tickets	**tři jízdenky** [trʒɪ ji:zdɛŋkɪ]
one-way	**jízdenka jedním směrem** [ji:zdɛŋka jɛdni:m smnerɛm]
round-trip	**zpáteční jízdenka** [zpa:tɛtʃni: ji:zdɛŋka]
first class	**první třída** [prvni: trʒi:da]
second class	**druhá třída** [druha: trʒi:da]
today	**dnes** [dnɛs]
tomorrow	**zítra** [zi:tra]
the day after tomorrow	**pozítří** [pozi:trʃi:]
in the morning	**dopoledne** [dopolɛdnɛ]
in the afternoon	**odpoledne** [otpolɛdnɛ]
in the evening	**večer** [vɛtʃɛr]

aisle seat

sedadlo u uličky
[sɛdadlo u ulɪtʃkɪ]

window seat

sedadlo u okna
[sɛdadlo u okna]

How much?

Kolik?
[kolɪk?]

Can I pay by credit card?

Můžu platit kreditní kartou?
[muːʒu platɪt krɛdɪtni: kartou?]

Bus

bus	**autobus** [autobus]
intercity bus	**meziměstský autobus** [mɛzɪmnestski: autobus]
bus stop	**autobusová zastávka** [autobusova: zasta:fka]
Where's the nearest bus stop?	**Kde je nejbližší autobusová zastávka?** [gdɛ jɛ nɛjblɪʒʃi: autobusova: zasta:fka?]
number (bus ~, etc.)	**číslo** [tʃi:slo]
Which bus do I take to get to …?	**Jakým autobusem se dostanu do …?** [jaki:m autobusɛm sɛ dostanu do …?]
Does this bus go to …?	**Jede tento autobus do …?** [jɛdɛ tɛnto autobus do …?]
How frequent are the buses?	**Jak často jezdí tento autobus?** [jak tʃasto jɛzdi: tɛnto autobus?]
every 15 minutes	**každých patnáct minut** [kaʒdi:x patna:tst mɪnut]
every half hour	**každou půlhodinu** [kaʒdou pu:lhodɪnu]
every hour	**každou hodinu** [kaʒdou hodɪnu]
several times a day	**několikrát za den** [nekolɪkra:t za dɛn]
… times a day	**… krát za den** [… kra:t za dɛn]
schedule	**jízdní řád** [ji:zdni: rʒa:t]
Where can I see the schedule?	**Kde se můžu podívat na jízdní řád?** [gdɛ sɛ mu:ʒu podi:vat na ji:zdni: rʒa:t?]
When is the next bus?	**Kdy jede příští autobus?** [gdɪ jɛdɛ prʒi:ʃti: autobus?]
When is the first bus?	**Kdy jede první autobus?** [gdɪ jɛdɛ prvni: autobus?]
When is the last bus?	**Kdy jede poslední autobus?** [gdɪ jɛdɛ poslɛdni: autobus?]
stop	**zastávka** [zasta:fka]
next stop	**příští zastávka** [prʃi:ʃti: zasta:fka]

last stop (terminus)

poslední zastávka
[poslɛdni: zasta:fka]

Stop here, please.

Zastavte tady, prosím.
[zastaftɛ tadɪ, prosi:m]

Excuse me, this is my stop.

Promiňte, já tady vystupuju.
[promɪnʲtɛ, ja: tadɪ vɪstupuju]

Train

train	**vlak** [vlak]
suburban train	**příměstský vlak** [prʒiːmnestskɪ vlak]
long-distance train	**dálkový vlak** [daːlkovi vlak]
train station	**vlakové nádraží** [vlakovɛ naːdraʒiː]
Excuse me, where is the exit to the platform?	**Promiňte, kde je vstup na nástupiště?** [promɪnʲtɛ, gdɛ jɛ vstup na naːstupɪʃte?]

Does this train go to …?	**Jede tento vlak do …?** [jɛdɛ tɛnto vlak do …?]
next train	**příští vlak** [prʃiːʃtiː vlak]
When is the next train?	**Kdy jede příští vlak?** [gdɪ jɛdɛ prʒiːʃtiː vlak?]
Where can I see the schedule?	**Kde se můžu podívat na jízdní řád?** [gdɛ sɛ muːʒu podiːvat na jiːzdni rʒaːt?]
From which platform?	**Ze kterého nástupiště?** [zɛ ktɛrɛːho naːstupɪʃte?]
When does the train arrive in …?	**Kdy přijede tento vlak do …?** [gdɪ prʃɪjɛdɛ tɛnto vlak do …?]

Please help me.	**Můžete mi prosím pomoct?** [muːʒetɛ mɪ prosiːm pomotst?]
I'm looking for my seat.	**Hledám své místo.** [hlɛdaːm svɛ miːsto]
We're looking for our seats.	**Hledáme svá místa.** [hlɛdaːmɛ sva miːsta]
My seat is taken.	**Moje místo je obsazeno.** [mojɛ miːsto jɛ opsazɛno]
Our seats are taken.	**Naše místa jsou obsazena.** [naʃɛ miːsta jsou opsazɛna]

I'm sorry but this is my seat.	**Promiňte, ale toto je moje místo.** [promɪnʲtɛ, alɛ toto jɛ mojɛ miːsto]
Is this seat taken?	**Je toto místo volné?** [jɛ toto miːsto volnɛː?]
May I sit here?	**Můžu si zde sednout?** [muːʒu sɪ zdɛ sɛdnout?]

On the train. Dialogue (No ticket)

Ticket, please. | **Jízdenku, prosím.**
[ji:zdɛŋku, prosi:m]

I don't have a ticket. | **Nemám jízdenku.**
[nɛma:m ji:zdɛŋku]

I lost my ticket. | **Ztratil jsem jízdenku.**
[stratɪl jsɛm ji:zdɛŋku]

I forgot my ticket at home. | **Zapomněl svou jízdenku doma.**
[zapomel svou ji:zdɛŋku doma]

You can buy a ticket from me. | **Jízdenku si můžete koupit u mě.**
[ji:zdɛŋku sɪ mu:ʒɛtɛ koupɪt u mne]

You will also have to pay a fine. | **Také budete muset zaplatit pokutu.**
[takɛ: budɛtɛ musɛt zaplatɪt pokutu]

Okay. | **Dobrá.**
[dobra:]

Where are you going? | **Kam jedete?**
[kam jɛdɛtɛ?]

I'm going to … | **Jedu do …**
[jɛdu do …]

How much? I don't understand. | **Kolik? Nerozumím.**
[kolɪk? nɛrozumi:m]

Write it down, please. | **Napište to, prosím.**
[napɪʃtɛ to, prosi:m]

Okay. Can I pay with a credit card? | **Dobrá. Můžu platit kreditní kartou?**
[dobra:. mu:ʒu platɪt krɛdɪtni: kartou?]

Yes, you can. | **Ano, můžete.**
[ano, mu:ʒɛtɛ]

Here's your receipt. | **Tady je vaše stvrzenka.**
[tadɪ jɛ vaʃɛ stvrzɛŋka]

Sorry about the fine. | **Omlouvám se za tu pokutu.**
[omlouva:m sɛ za tu pokutu]

That's okay. It was my fault. | **To je v pořádku. Je to moje chyba.**
[to jɛ v porʒa:tku. jɛ to mojɛ xɪba]

Enjoy your trip. | **Příjemnou cestu.**
[prʒi:jɛmnou tsɛstu]

Taxi

taxi
taxík
[taksi:k]

taxi driver
taxikář
[taksɪka:rʒ]

to catch a taxi
chytit si taxík
[xɪtɪt sɪ taksi:k]

taxi stand
stanoviště taxíků
[stanovɪʃte taksi:ku:]

Where can I get a taxi?
Kde můžu sehnat taxík?
[gdɛ mu:ʒu sɛhnat taksi:k?]

to call a taxi
volat taxík
[volat taksi:k]

I need a taxi.
Potřebuju taxík.
[potrʒɛbuju taksi:k]

Right now.
Hned teď.
[hnɛt tɛtʲ]

What is your address (location)?
Jaká je vaše adresa?
[jaka: jɛ vaʃɛ adrɛsa?]

My address is …
Moje adresa je …
[mojɛ adrɛsa jɛ …]

Your destination?
Váš cíl?
[va:ʃ tsi:l?]

Excuse me, …
Promiňte, …
[promɪnʲtɛ, …]

Are you available?
Jste volný?
[jstɛ volni:?]

How much is it to get to …?
Kolik to stojí do …?
[kolɪk to stoji: do …?]

Do you know where it is?
Víte, kde to je?
[vi:tɛ, gdɛ to jɛ?]

Airport, please.
Na letiště, prosím.
[na lɛtɪʃte, prosi:m]

Stop here, please.
Zastavte tady, prosím.
[zastaftɛ tadɪ, prosi:m]

It's not here.
To není tady.
[to nɛni: tadɪ]

This is the wrong address.
To je nesprávná adresa.
[to jɛ nɛspra:vna: adrɛsa]

Turn left.
Zabočte doleva.
[zabotʃtɛ dolɛva]

Turn right.
Zabočte doprava.
[zabotʃtɛ doprava]

How much do I owe you?

Kolik vám dlužím?
[kolɪk vaːm dluʒiːm?]

I'd like a receipt, please.

Chtěl /Chtěla/ bych stvrzenku, prosím.
[xtel /xtela/ bɪx stvrzɛŋku, prosiːm]

Keep the change.

Drobné si nechte.
[drobnɛ: sɪ nɛxtɛ]

Would you please wait for me?

Můžete tady na mě počkat?
[muːʒetɛ tadɪ na mne potʃkat?]

five minutes

pět minut
[pet mɪnut]

ten minutes

deset minut
[dɛsɛt mɪnut]

fifteen minutes

patnáct minut
[patnaːtst mɪnut]

twenty minutes

dvacet minut
[dvatsɛt mɪnut]

half an hour

půl hodiny
[puːl hodɪnɪ]

Hotel

Hello.	**Dobrý den.** [dobri: dɛn]
My name is ...	**Jmenuju se ...** [jmɛnuju sɛ ...]
I have a reservation.	**Mám tady rezervaci.** [ma:m tadɪ rɛzɛrvatsɪ]
I need ...	**Potřebuju ...** [potrʒɛbuju ...]
a single room	**jednolůžkový pokoj** [jɛdnolu:ʃkovi pokoj]
a double room	**dvoulůžkový pokoj** [dvoulu:ʃkovi pokoj]
How much is that?	**Kolik to stojí?** [kolɪk to stoji:?]
That's a bit expensive.	**To je trochu drahé.** [to jɛ troxu drahɛ:]
Do you have anything else?	**Máte nějaké další možnosti?** [ma:tɛ nejakɛ: dalʃi: moʒnostɪ?]
I'll take it.	**To si vezmu.** [to sɪ vɛzmu]
I'll pay in cash.	**Budu platit v hotovosti.** [budu platɪt v hotovostɪ]
I've got a problem.	**Mám problém.** [ma:m problɛ:m]
My ... is broken.	**... je rozbitý /rozbitá/.** [... jɛ rozbɪti: /rozbɪta:/]
My ... is out of order.	**... je mimo provoz.** [... jɛ mɪmo provoz]
TV	**Můj televizor ...** [mu:j tɛlɛvɪzor ...]
air conditioner	**Moje klimatizace ...** [mojɛ klɪmatɪzatsɛ ...]
tap	**Můj kohoutek ...** [mu:j kohoutɛk ...]
shower	**Moje sprcha ...** [mojɛ sprxa ...]
sink	**Můj dřez ...** [mu:j drʒɛz ...]
safe	**Můj sejf ...** [mu:j sɛjf ...]

door lock	**Můj zámek ...** [muːj zaːmɛk ...]
electrical outlet	**Moje elektrická zásuvka ...** [mojɛ ɛlɛktrɪtska: zaːsufka ...]
hairdryer	**Můj fén ...** [muːj fɛːn ...]

I don't have ...	**Nemám ...** [nɛmaːm ...]
water	**vodu** [vodu]
light	**světlo** [svetlo]
electricity	**elektřinu** [ɛlɛktrʒɪnu]

Can you give me ...?	**Můžete mi dát ...?** [muːʒetɛ mɪ daːt ...?]
a towel	**ručník** [rutʃniːk]
a blanket	**přikrývku** [prʒɪkriːfku]
slippers	**bačkory** [batʃkorɪ]
a robe	**župan** [ʒupan]
shampoo	**šampón** [ʃampón]
soap	**mýdlo** [miːdlo]

I'd like to change rooms.	**Chtěl bych vyměnit pokoje.** [xtel bɪx vɪmnenɪt pokojɛ]
I can't find my key.	**Nemůžu najít klíč.** [nɛmuːʒu najiːt kliːtʃ]
Could you open my room, please?	**Můžete mi otevřít pokoj, prosím?** [muːʒetɛ mɪ otɛvrʒiːt pokoj, prosiːm?]
Who's there?	**Kdo je tam?** [gdo jɛ tam?]
Come in!	**Vstupte!** [vstuptɛ!]
Just a minute!	**Minutku!** [mɪnutku!]
Not right now, please.	**Teď ne, prosím.** [tɛtʲ nɛ, prosiːm]

Come to my room, please.	**Pojďte do mého pokoje, prosím.** [pojdʲtɛ do mɛːho pokojɛ, prosiːm]
I'd like to order food service.	**Chtěl bych si objednat jídlo.** [xtel bɪx sɪ objednat jiːdlo]
My room number is ...	**Číslo mého pokoje je ...** [tʃiːslo mɛːho pokojɛ jɛ ...]

I'm leaving …

Odjíždím …
[odjiːʒdiːm …]

We're leaving …

Odjíždíme …
[odjiːʒdiːmɛ …]

right now

hned teď
[hnɛt tɛtʲ]

this afternoon

dnes odpoledne
[dnɛs otpolɛdnɛ]

tonight

dnes večer
[dnɛs vɛtʃɛr]

tomorrow

zítra
[ziːtra]

tomorrow morning

zítra dopoledne
[ziːtra dopolɛdnɛ]

tomorrow evening

zítra večer
[ziːtra vɛtʃɛr]

the day after tomorrow

pozítří
[poziːtrʃiː]

I'd like to pay.

Chtěl bych zaplatit.
[xtel bɪx zaplatɪt]

Everything was wonderful.

Všechno bylo skvělé.
[vʃɛxno bɪlo skvelɛː]

Where can I get a taxi?

Kde můžu sehnat taxík?
[gdɛ muːʒu sɛhnat taksiːk?]

Would you call a taxi for me, please?

Můžete mi zavolat taxík, prosím?
[muːʒetɛ mɪ zavolat taksiːk, prosiːm?]

Restaurant

Can I look at the menu, please?

Můžu se podívat na jídelní lístek, prosím?
[muːʒu sɛ podiːvat na jiːdɛlniː liːstɛk, prosiːm?]

Table for one.

Stůl pro jednoho.
[stuːl pro jɛdnoho]

There are two (three, four) of us.

Jsme dva (tři, čtyři).
[jsmɛ dva (trʒɪ, tʃtɪrʒɪ)]

Smoking

Kuřáci
[kurʒaːtsɪ]

No smoking

Nekuřáci
[nɛkurʒaːtsɪ]

Excuse me! (addressing a waiter)

Promiňte!
[promɪɲtɛ!]

menu

jídelní lístek
[jiːdɛlniː liːstɛk]

wine list

vinný lístek
[vɪnniː liːstɛk]

The menu, please.

Jídelní lístek, prosím.
[jiːdɛlniː liːstɛk, prosiːm]

Are you ready to order?

Vybrali jste si?
[vɪbralɪ jstɛ sɪ?]

What will you have?

Co si dáte?
[tso sɪ daːtɛ?]

I'll have ...

Dám si ...
[daːm sɪ ...]

I'm a vegetarian.

Jsem vegetarián.
[jsɛm vɛgɛtariaːn]

meat

maso
[maso]

fish

ryba
[rɪba]

vegetables

zelenina
[zɛlɛnɪna]

Do you have vegetarian dishes?

Máte vegetariánská jídla?
[maːtɛ vɛgɛtariaːnska jiːdla?]

I don't eat pork.

Nejím vepřové.
[nɛjiːm vɛprʃovɛː]

Band-Aid

On /ona/ nejí maso.
[on /ona/ nɛjiː maso]

I am allergic to ...

Jsem alergický /alergická/ na ...
[jsɛm alɛrgɪtskiː /alɛrgɪtska:/ na ...]

Would you please bring me ...

Přinesl byste mi prosím ...
[prʒɪnɛsl bɪstɛ mɪ prosi:m ...]

salt | pepper | sugar

sůl | pepř | cukr
[su:l | pɛprʒ | tsukr]

coffee | tea | dessert

kávu | čaj | zákusek
[ka:vu | tʃaj | za:kusɛk]

water | sparkling | plain

vodu | perlivou | neperlivou
[vodu | pɛrlɪvou | nɛpɛrlɪvou]

a spoon | fork | knife

lžíci | vidličku | nůž
[lʒi:tsɪ | vɪdlɪtʃku | nu:ʒ]

a plate | napkin

talíř | ubrousek
[tali:rʒ | ubrousɛk]

Enjoy your meal!

Dobrou chuť!
[dobrou xutʃ!]

One more, please.

Ještě jednou, prosím.
[jɛʃte jɛdnou, prosi:m]

It was very delicious.

Bylo to výborné.
[bɪlo to vi:bornɛ:]

check | change | tip

účet | drobné | spropitné
[u:tʃɛt | drobnɛ: | spropɪtnɛ:]

Check, please.
(Could I have the check, please?)

Účet, prosím.
[u:tʃɛt, prosi:m]

Can I pay by credit card?

Můžu platit kreditní kartou?
[mu:ʒu platɪt krɛdɪtni: kartou?]

I'm sorry, there's a mistake here.

Omlouvám se, ale tady je chyba.
[omlouva:m sɛ, alɛ tadɪ jɛ xɪba]

Shopping

Can I help you?	**Co si přejete?** [tso sɪ prʒɛjɛtɛ?]
Do you have …?	**Máte …?** [maːtɛ …?]
I'm looking for …	**Hledám …** [hlɛdaːm …]
I need …	**Potřebuju …** [potrʒɛbuju …]
I'm just looking.	**Jen se dívám.** [jɛn sɛ diːvaːm]
We're just looking.	**Jen se díváme.** [jɛn sɛ diːvaːmɛ]
I'll come back later.	**Vrátím se později.** [vraːtiːm sɛ pozdɛjɪ]
We'll come back later.	**Vrátíme se později.** [vraːtiːmɛ sɛ pozdɛjɪ]
discounts | sale	**slevy | výprodej** [slɛvɪ | viːprodɛj]
Would you please show me …	**Můžete mi prosím ukázat …** [muːʒetɛ mɪ prosiːm ukaːzat …]
Would you please give me …	**Můžete mi prosím dát …** [muːʒetɛ mɪ prosiːm daːt …]
Can I try it on?	**Můžu si to vyzkoušet?** [muːʒu sɪ to vɪskouʃɛt?]
Excuse me, where's the fitting room?	**Promiňte, kde je zkušební kabinka?** [promɪnʲtɛ, gdɛ jɛ skuʃɛbniː kabɪŋka?]
Which color would you like?	**Jakou byste chtěl /chtěla/ barvu?** [jakou bɪstɛ xtel /xtela/ barvu?]
size | length	**velikost | délku** [vɛlɪkost | dɛːlku]
How does it fit?	**Jak vám to sedí?** [jak vaːm to sɛdiː?]
How much is it?	**Kolik to stojí?** [kolɪk to stojiː?]
That's too expensive.	**To je příliš drahé.** [to jɛ prʃiːlɪʃ drahɛː]
I'll take it.	**Vezmu si to.** [vɛzmu sɪ to]
Excuse me, where do I pay?	**Promiňte, kde můžu zaplatit?** [promɪnʲtɛ, gdɛ muːʒu zaplatɪt?]

Will you pay in cash or credit card? **Budete platit v hotovosti nebo kreditní kartou?**
[budɛtɛ platɪt v hotovostɪ nɛbo krɛdɪtni: kartou?]

In cash | with credit card **v hotovosti | kreditní kartou**
[v hotovostɪ | krɛdɪtni: kartou]

Do you want the receipt? **Chcete stvrzenku?**
[xtsɛtɛ stvrzɛŋku?]

Yes, please. **Ano, prosím.**
[ano, prosi:m]

No, it's OK. **Ne, to je dobré.**
[nɛ, to jɛ dobrɛ:]

Thank you. Have a nice day! **Děkuji. Hezký den.**
[dekujɪ. hɛski: dɛn]

In town

Excuse me, …	**Promiňte, prosím.** [promɪɲtɛ, prosiːm]
I'm looking for …	**Hledám …** [hlɛdaːm …]
the subway	**metro** [mɛtro]
my hotel	**svůj hotel** [svuːj hotɛl]
the movie theater	**kino** [kɪno]
a taxi stand	**stanoviště taxíků** [stanovɪʃtɛ taksiːkuː]
an ATM	**bankomat** [baŋkomat]
a foreign exchange office	**směnárnu** [smnenaːrnu]
an internet café	**internetovou kavárnu** [ɪntɛrnɛtovou kavaːrnu]
… street	**… ulici** [… ulɪtsɪ]
this place	**toto místo** [toto miːsto]
Do you know where … is?	**Nevíte, kde je …?** [nɛviːtɛ, gdɛ jɛ …?]
Which street is this?	**Jaká je toto ulice?** [jaka: jɛ toto ulɪtsɛ?]
Show me where we are right now.	**Ukažte mi, kde teď jsme.** [ukaʃtɛ mɪ, gdɛ tɛdʲ jsmɛ]
Can I get there on foot?	**Dostanu se tam pěšky?** [dostanu sɛ tam pɛʃkɪ?]
Do you have a map of the city?	**Máte mapu tohoto města?** [ma:tɛ mapu tohoto mnesta?]
How much is a ticket to get in?	**Kolik stojí vstupenka?** [kolɪk stoji: vstupɛŋka?]
Can I take pictures here?	**Můžu tady fotit?** [mu:ʒu tadɪ fotɪt?]
Are you open?	**Máte otevřeno?** [ma:tɛ otɛvrʒɛno?]

When do you open?   **Kdy otvíráte?**
                                     [gdɪ otviːraːtɛ?]

When do you close?   **Kdy zavíráte?**
                                     [gdɪ zaviːraːtɛ?]

Money

money	**peníze** [pɛni:zɛ]
cash	**hotovost** [hotovost]
paper money	**papírové peníze** [papi:rovɛ: pɛni:zɛ]
loose change	**drobné** [drobnɛ:]
check | change | tip	**účet | drobné | spropitné** [u:tʃɛt | drobnɛ: | spropɪtnɛ:]
credit card	**kreditní karta** [krɛdɪtni: karta]
wallet	**peněženka** [pɛnɛʒɛŋka]
to buy	**koupit** [koupɪt]
to pay	**platit** [platɪt]
fine	**pokuta** [pokuta]
free	**zdarma** [zdarma]
Where can I buy ...?	**Kde dostanu koupit ...?** [gdɛ dostanu koupɪt ...?]
Is the bank open now?	**Je teď otevřená banka?** [jɛ tɛdʲ otɛvrʒɛna: baŋka?]
When does it open?	**Kdy otvírají?** [gdɪ otvi:raji:?]
When does it close?	**Kdy zavírají?** [gdɪ zavi:raji:?]
How much?	**Kolik?** [kolɪk?]
How much is this?	**Kolik to stojí?** [kolɪk to stoji:?]
That's too expensive.	**To je příliš drahé.** [to jɛ prʃi:lɪʃ drahɛ:]
Excuse me, where do I pay?	**Promiňte, kde můžu zaplatit?** [promɪnʲtɛ, gdɛ mu:ʒu zaplatɪt?]
Check, please.	**Účet, prosím.** [u:tʃɛt, prosi:m]

Can I pay by credit card?

Můžu platit kreditní kartou?
[muːʒu platɪt krɛdɪtniː kartou?]

Is there an ATM here?

Je tady bankomat?
[jɛ tadɪ baŋkomat?]

I'm looking for an ATM.

Hledám bankomat.
[hlɛdaːm baŋkomat]

I'm looking for a foreign exchange office.

Hledám směnárnu.
[hlɛdaːm smnenaːrnu]

I'd like to change …

Chtěl bych si vyměnit …
[xtel bɪx sɪ vɪmnenɪt …]

What is the exchange rate?

Jaký je kurz?
[jakiː jɛ kurs?]

Do you need my passport?

Potřebujete můj pas?
[potrʒɛbujɛtɛ muːj pas?]

Time

What time is it?	**Kolik je hodin?** [kolɪk jɛ hodɪn?]
When?	**Kdy?** [gdɪ?]
At what time?	**V kolik hodin?** [v kolɪk hodɪn?]
now | later | after …	**teď | později | po …** [tɛdʲ | pozdejɪ | po …]
one o'clock	**jedna hodina** [jɛdna hodɪna]
one fifteen	**čtvrt na dvě** [tʃtvrt na dve]
one thirty	**půl druhé** [puːl druhɛ:]
one forty-five	**tři čtvrtě na dvě** [trʒɪ tʃtvrte na dve]
one | two | three	**jedna | dvě | tři** [jɛdna | dve | trʒɪ]
four | five | six	**čtyři | pět | šest** [tʃtɪrʒɪ | pet | ʃest]
seven | eight | nine	**sedm | osm | devět** [sɛdm | osm | dɛvet]
ten | eleven | twelve	**deset | jedenáct | dvanáct** [dɛsɛt | jɛdɛnaːtst | dvanaːtst]
in …	**za …** [za …]
five minutes	**pět minut** [pet mɪnut]
ten minutes	**deset minut** [dɛsɛt mɪnut]
fifteen minutes	**patnáct minut** [patnaːtst mɪnut]
twenty minutes	**dvacet minut** [dvatsɛt mɪnut]
half an hour	**půl hodiny** [puːl hodɪnɪ]
an hour	**hodinu** [hodɪnu]

in the morning	**dopoledne**
	[dopolɛdnɛ]
early in the morning	**brzy ráno**
	[brzɪ raːno]
this morning	**dnes dopoledne**
	[dnɛs dopolɛdnɛ]
tomorrow morning	**zítra dopoledne**
	[ziːtra dopolɛdnɛ]

in the middle of the day	**v poledne**
	[v polɛdnɛ]
in the afternoon	**odpoledne**
	[otpolɛdnɛ]
in the evening	**večer**
	[vɛtʃɛr]
tonight	**dnes večer**
	[dnɛs vɛtʃɛr]

at night	**v noci**
	[v notsɪ]
yesterday	**včera**
	[vtʃɛra]
today	**dnes**
	[dnɛs]
tomorrow	**zítra**
	[ziːtra]
the day after tomorrow	**pozítří**
	[poziːtrʃiː]

What day is it today?	**Kolikátého je dnes?**
	[kolɪkaːtɛːho jɛ dnɛs?]
It's ...	**Dnes je …**
	[dnɛs jɛ …]
Monday	**pondělí**
	[pondeliː]
Tuesday	**úterý**
	[uːtɛriː]
Wednesday	**středa**
	[strʒɛda]

Thursday	**čtvrtek**
	[tʃtvrtɛk]
Friday	**pátek**
	[paːtɛk]
Saturday	**sobota**
	[sobota]
Sunday	**neděle**
	[nɛdelɛ]

Greetings. Introductions

Hello. | **Dobrý den.**
[dobri: dɛn]

Pleased to meet you. | **Těší mě, že vás poznávám.**
[teʃi: mne, ʒe va:s pozna:va:m]

Me too. | **Mě také.**
[mne takɛ:]

I'd like you to meet ... | **Rád /Ráda/ bych**
vás seznámil /seznámila/ ...
[ra:d /ra:da/ bɪx
va:s sɛzna:mɪl /sɛzna:mɪla/ ...]

Nice to meet you. | **Těší mě.**
[teʃi: mne]

How are you? | **Jak se máte?**
[jak sɛ ma:tɛ?]

My name is ... | **Jmenuju se ...**
[jmɛnuju sɛ ...]

His name is ... | **On se jmenuje ...**
[on sɛ jmɛnujɛ ...]

Her name is ... | **Ona se jmenuje ...**
[ona sɛ jmɛnujɛ ...]

What's your name? | **Jak se jmenujete?**
[jak sɛ jmɛnujɛtɛ?]

What's his name? | **Jak se jmenuje?**
[jak sɛ jmɛnujɛ?]

What's her name? | **Jak se jmenuje?**
[jak sɛ jmɛnujɛ?]

What's your last name? | **Jaké je vaše příjmení?**
[jakɛ: jɛ vaʃɛ prʒi:jmɛni:?]

You can call me ... | **Můžete mi říkat ...**
[mu:ʒetɛ mɪ rʒi:kat ...]

Where are you from? | **Odkud jste?**
[otkut jstɛ?]

I'm from ... | **Jsem z ...**
[jsɛm s ...]

What do you do for a living? | **Čím jste?**
[tʃi:m jstɛ?]

Who is this? | **Kdo to je?**
[gdo to jɛ?]

Who is he? | **Kdo je on?**
[gdo jɛ on?]

Who is she?	**Kdo je ona?**
	[gdo jɛ ona?]
Who are they?	**Kdo jsou oni?**
	[gdo jsou onɪ?]

This is …	**To je …**
	[to jɛ …]
my friend (masc.)	**můj přítel**
	[muːj prʃiːtɛl]
my friend (fem.)	**moje přítelkyně**
	[mojɛ prʃiːtɛlkɪnɛ]
my husband	**můj manžel**
	[muːj manʒel]
my wife	**moje manželka**
	[mojɛ manʒelka]

my father	**můj otec**
	[muːj otɛts]
my mother	**moje matka**
	[mojɛ matka]
my brother	**můj bratr**
	[muːj bratr]
my sister	**moje sestra**
	[mojɛ sɛstra]
my son	**můj syn**
	[muːj sɪn]
my daughter	**moje dcera**
	[mojɛ dtsɛra]

This is our son.	**To je náš syn.**
	[to jɛ naːʃ sɪn]
This is our daughter.	**To je naše dcera.**
	[to jɛ naʃɛ dtsɛra]
These are my children.	**To jsou moje děti.**
	[to jsou mojɛ detɪ]
These are our children.	**To jsou naše děti.**
	[to jsou naʃɛ detɪ]

Farewells

Good bye!	**Na shledanou!** [na sxlɛdanou!]
Bye! (inform.)	**Ahoj!** [ahoj!]
See you tomorrow.	**Uvidíme se zítra.** [uvɪdiːmɛ sɛ ziːtra]
See you soon.	**Brzy ahoj.** [brzɪ ahoj]
See you at seven.	**Ahoj v sedm.** [ahoj v sɛdm]
Have fun!	**Hezkou zábavu!** [hɛskou zaːbavu!]
Talk to you later.	**Promluvíme si později.** [promluviːmɛ sɪ pozdejɪ]
Have a nice weekend.	**Hezký víkend.** [hɛskɪ viːkɛnt]
Good night.	**Dobrou noc.** [dobrou nots]
It's time for me to go.	**Už musím jít.** [uʒ musiːm jiːt]
I have to go.	**Musím jít.** [musiːm jiːt]
I will be right back.	**Hned se vrátím.** [hnɛt sɛ vraːtiːm]
It's late.	**Je pozdě.** [jɛ pozde]
I have to get up early.	**Musím brzy vstávat.** [musiːm brzɪ vstaːvat]
I'm leaving tomorrow.	**Zítra odjíždím.** [ziːtra odjiːʒdiːm]
We're leaving tomorrow.	**Zítra odjíždíme.** [ziːtra odjiːʒdiːmɛ]
Have a nice trip!	**Hezký výlet!** [hɛskɪ vɪlɛt!]
It was nice meeting you.	**Jsem rád /ráda/, že jsem vás poznal /poznala/.** [jsɛm raːd /raːda/, ʒe jsɛm vaːs poznal /poznala/]

It was nice talking to you.

Rád /Ráda/ jsem si s vámi popovídal /popovídala/.
[ra:d /ra:da/ jsɛm sɪ s va:mɪ popoviːdal /popoviːdala/]

Thanks for everything.

Děkuji vám za všechno.
[dekujɪ va:m za vʃɛxno]

I had a very good time.

Měl /Měla/ jsem se moc dobře.
[mnel /mnela/ jsɛm sɛ mots dobrʒɛ]

We had a very good time.

Měli /Měly/ jsme se moc dobře.
[mnelɪ /mnelɪ/ jsmɛ sɛ mots dobrʒɛ]

It was really great.

Bylo to fakt skvělé.
[bɪlo to fakt skvelɛː]

I'm going to miss you.

Bude se mi po tobě stýskat.
[budɛ sɛ mɪ po tobe stiːskat]

We're going to miss you.

Bude se nám po vás stýskat.
[budɛ sɛ na:m po va:s stiːskat]

Good luck!

Hodně štěstí!
[hodne ʃtesti:!]

Say hi to …

Pozdravuj …
[pozdravuj …]

Foreign language

I don't understand.	**Nerozumím.** [nɛrozumi:m]
Write it down, please.	**Napište to, prosím.** [napɪʃtɛ to, prosi:m]
Do you speak ...?	**Mluvíte ...?** [mluvi:tɛ ...?]
I speak a little bit of ...	**Mluvím trochu ...** [mluvi:m troxu ...]
English	**anglicky** [anglɪtskɪ]
Turkish	**turecky** [turɛtskɪ]
Arabic	**arabsky** [arapskɪ]
French	**francouzsky** [frantsouskɪ]
German	**německy** [nemɛtskɪ]
Italian	**italsky** [ɪtalskɪ]
Spanish	**španělsky** [ʃpanelskɪ]
Portuguese	**portugalsky** [portugalskɪ]
Chinese	**čínsky** [tʃi:nskɪ]
Japanese	**japonsky** [japonskɪ]
Can you repeat that, please.	**Můžete to prosím zopakovat.** [mu:ʒetɛ to prosi:m zopakovat]
I understand.	**Rozumím.** [rozumi:m]
I don't understand.	**Nerozumím.** [nɛrozumi:m]
Please speak more slowly.	**Mluvte prosím pomalu.** [mluftɛ prosi:m pomalu]
Is that correct? (Am I saying it right?)	**Je to správně?** [jɛ to spra:vne?]
What is this? (What does this mean?)	**Co to je?** [tso to jɛ?]

Apologies

Excuse me, please.	**Promiňte, prosím.** [promɪnɪtɛ, prosiːm]
I'm sorry.	**Omlouvám se.** [omlouvaːm sɛ]
I'm really sorry.	**Je mi to opravdu líto.** [jɛ mɪ to opravdu liːto]
Sorry, it's my fault.	**Omlouvám se, je to moje chyba.** [omlouvaːm sɛ, jɛ to mojɛ xɪba]
My mistake.	**Moje chyba.** [mojɛ xɪba]

May I ...?	**Můžu ...?** [muːʒu ...?]
Do you mind if I ...?	**Nevadilo by vám, kdybych ...?** [nɛvadɪlo bɪ vaːm, gdɪbɪx ...?]
It's OK.	**Nic se nestalo.** [nɪts sɛ nɛstalo]
It's all right.	**To je v pořádku.** [to jɛ v porʒaːtku]
Don't worry about it.	**Tím se netrapte.** [tiːm sɛ nɛtraptɛ]

Agreement

Yes.	**Ano.** [ano]
Yes, sure.	**Ano, jistě.** [ano, jɪste]
OK (Good!)	**Dobrá.** [dobra:]
Very well.	**Dobře.** [dobrʒɛ]
Certainly!	**Samozřejmě!** [samozrʒɛjmne!]
I agree.	**Souhlasím.** [souhlasi:m]
That's correct.	**To je správně.** [to jɛ spra:vne]
That's right.	**To je v pořádku.** [to jɛ v porʒa:tku]
You're right.	**Máte pravdu.** [ma:tɛ pravdu]
I don't mind.	**Nevadí mi to.** [nɛvadi: mɪ to]
Absolutely right.	**To je naprosto správně.** [to jɛ naprosto spra:vne]
It's possible.	**Je to možné.** [jɛ to moʒnɛ:]
That's a good idea.	**To je dobrý nápad.** [to jɛ dobri: na:pat]
I can't say no.	**Nemůžu říct ne.** [nɛmu:ʒu rʒi:tst nɛ]
I'd be happy to.	**Hrozně rád /ráda/.** [hrozne ra:d /ra:da/]
With pleasure.	**S radostí.** [s radosti:]

Refusal. Expressing doubt

No.	**Ne.** [nɛ]
Certainly not.	**Určitě ne.** [urtʃɪte nɛ]
I don't agree.	**Nesouhlasím.** [nɛsouhlasi:m]
I don't think so.	**Myslím, že ne.** [mɪsli:m, ʒe nɛ]
It's not true.	**To není pravda.** [to nɛni: pravda]
You are wrong.	**Mýlíte se.** [mɪli:tɛ sɛ]
I think you are wrong.	**Myslím, že se mýlíte.** [mɪsli:m, ʒe sɛ mi:li:tɛ]
I'm not sure.	**Nejsem si jist /jista/.** [nɛjsɛm sɪ jɪst /jɪsta/]
It's impossible.	**To je nemožné.** [to jɛ nɛmoʒnɛ:]
Nothing of the kind (sort)!	**Nic takového!** [nɪts takovɛ:ho!]
The exact opposite.	**Přesně naopak.** [prʃɛsne naopak]
I'm against it.	**Jsem proti.** [jsɛm protɪ]
I don't care.	**Je mi to jedno.** [jɛ mɪ to jɛdno]
I have no idea.	**Nemám ani ponětí.** [nɛma:m anɪ poneti:]
I doubt it.	**To pochybuju.** [to poxɪbuju]
Sorry, I can't.	**Bohužel, nemůžu.** [bohuʒel, nɛmu:ʒu]
Sorry, I don't want to.	**Bohužel, nechci.** [bohuʒel, nɛxtsɪ]
Thank you, but I don't need this.	**Děkuju, ale to já nepotřebuju.** [dekuju, alɛ to ja: nɛpotrʒɛbuju]
It's getting late.	**Už je pozdě.** [uʒ jɛ pozde]

I have to get up early.

Musím brzy vstávat.
[musi:m brzɪ vsta:vat]

I don't feel well.

Necítím se dobře.
[nɛtsi:ti:m sɛ dobrʒɛ]

Expressing gratitude

Thank you.	**Děkuju.** [dekuju]
Thank you very much.	**Děkuju mockrát.** [dekuju motskra:t]
I really appreciate it.	**Opravdu si toho vážím.** [opravdu sɪ toho va:ʒi:m]
I'm really grateful to you.	**Jsem vám opravdu vděčný /vděčná/.** [jsɛm va:m opravdu vdetʃni: /vdetʃna:/]
We are really grateful to you.	**Jsme vám opravdu vděční.** [jsmɛ va:m opravdu vdetʃni:]
Thank you for your time.	**Děkuju za váš čas.** [dekuju za va:ʃ tʃas]
Thanks for everything.	**Děkuju za všechno.** [dekuju za vʃɛxno]
Thank you for …	**Děkuju za …** [dekuju za …]
your help	**vaši pomoc** [vaʃɪ pomots]
a nice time	**příjemně strávený čas** [prʒi:jɛme stra:vɛnɪ tʃas]
a wonderful meal	**skvělé jídlo** [skvelɛ ji:dlo]
a pleasant evening	**příjemný večer** [prʒi:jɛmnɪ vɛtʃɛr]
a wonderful day	**nádherný den** [na:dhɛrni: dɛn]
an amazing journey	**úžasnou cestu** [u:ʒasnou tsɛstu]
Don't mention it.	**To nestojí za řeč.** [to nɛstoji: za rʒɛtʃ]
You are welcome.	**Není zač.** [nɛni: zatʃ]
Any time.	**Je mi potěšením.** [jɛ mɪ poteʃɛni:m]
My pleasure.	**S radostí.** [s radosti:]
Forget it.	**To nestojí za řeč.** [to nɛstoji: za rʒɛtʃ]
Don't worry about it.	**Tím se netrapte.** [ti:m sɛ nɛtraptɛ]

Congratulations. Best wishes

Congratulations!
Blahopřeju!
[blahoprʒɛju!]

Happy birthday!
Všechno nejlepší k narozeninám!
[vʃɛxno nɛjlɛpʃi: k narozɛnɪna:m!]

Merry Christmas!
Veselé Vánoce!
[vɛsɛlɛ: va:notsɛ!]

Happy New Year!
Šťastný nový rok!
[ʃtˈastni: novi: rok!]

Happy Easter!
Veselé Velikonoce!
[vɛsɛlɛ: vɛlɪkonotsɛ!]

Happy Hanukkah!
Šťastnou Chanuku!
[ʃtˈastnou xanuku!]

I'd like to propose a toast.
Chtěl /Chtěla/ bych pronést přípitek.
[xtel /xtela/ bɪx pronɛ:st prʒi:pɪtɛk]

Cheers!
Na zdraví!
[na zdravi:!]

Let's drink to …!
Pojďme se napít na …!
[pojdˈmɛ sɛ napi:t na …!]

To our success!
Na náš úspěch!
[na na:ʃ u:spex!]

To your success!
Na váš úspěch!
[na va:ʃ u:spex!]

Good luck!
Hodně štěstí!
[hodne ʃtesti:!]

Have a nice day!
Hezký den!
[hɛski: dɛn!]

Have a good holiday!
Hezkou dovolenou!
[hɛskou dovolɛnou!]

Have a safe journey!
Šťastnou cestu!
[ʃtˈastnou tsɛstu!]

I hope you get better soon!
Doufám, že se brzy uzdravíte!
[doufa:m, ʒe sɛ brzɪ uzdravi:tɛ!]

Socializing

Why are you sad?

Proč jste smutný /smutná/?
[protʃ jstɛ smutni: /smutna:/?]

Smile! Cheer up!

Usmějte se! Hlavu vzhůru!
[usmnejtɛ sɛ! hlavu vzhu:ru!]

Are you free tonight?

Máte dnes večer čas?
[ma:tɛ dnɛs vɛtʃɛr tʃas?]

May I offer you a drink?

Můžu vám nabídnout něco k pití?
[mu:ʒu va:m nabi:dnout netso k pɪti:?]

Would you like to dance?

Smím prosít?
[smi:m prosi:t?]

Let's go to the movies.

Nechcete jít do kina?
[nɛxtsɛtɛ ji:t do kɪna?]

May I invite you to ...?

Můžu vás pozvat ...?
[mu:ʒu va:s pozvat ...?]

a restaurant

do restaurace
[do rɛstauratsɛ]

the movies

do kina
[do kɪna]

the theater

do divadla
[do dɪvadla]

go for a walk

na procházku
[na proxa:sku]

At what time?

V kolik hodin?
[v kolɪk hodɪn?]

tonight

dnes večer
[dnɛs vɛtʃɛr]

at six

v šest
[v ʃɛst]

at seven

v sedm
[v sɛdm]

at eight

v osm
[v osm]

at nine

v devět
[v dɛvet]

Do you like it here?

Líbí se vám tady?
[li:bi: sɛ va:m tadɪ?]

Are you here with someone?

Jste tady s někým?
[jstɛ tadɪ s neki:m?]

I'm with my friend.

Jsem tady s přítelem /přítelkyní/.
[jsɛm tadɪ s prʒi:tɛlɛm /prʒi:tɛlkɪni:/]

I'm with my friends.
Jsem tady s přáteli.
[jsɛm tadɪ s prʒaːtɛlɪ]

No, I'm alone.
Ne, jsem tady sám /sama/.
[nɛ, jsɛm tadɪ saːm /sama/]

Do you have a boyfriend?
Máš přítele?
[maːʃ prʃiːtɛlɛ?]

I have a boyfriend.
Mám přítele.
[maːm prʃiːtɛlɛ]

Do you have a girlfriend?
Máš přítelkyni?
[maːʃ prʃiːtɛlkɪnɪ?]

I have a girlfriend.
Mám přítelkyni.
[maːm prʃiːtɛlkɪnɪ]

Can I see you again?
Můžu tě zase vidět?
[muːʒu te zasɛ vɪdet?]

Can I call you?
Můžu ti zavolat?
[muːʒu tɪ zavolat?]

Call me. (Give me a call.)
Zavolej mi.
[zavolɛj mɪ]

What's your number?
Jaké je tvoje číslo?
[jakɛ jɛ tvojɛ tʃiːslo?]

I miss you.
Stýská se mi po tobě.
[stiːska sɛ mɪ po tobe]

You have a beautiful name.
Máte krásné jméno.
[maːtɛ kraːsnɛː jmɛːno]

I love you.
Miluju tě.
[mɪluju te]

Will you marry me?
Vezmeš si mě?
[vɛzmɛʃ sɪ mne?]

You're kidding!
Děláte si legraci!
[delaːtɛ sɪ lɛgratsɪ!]

I'm just kidding.
Žertoval /Žertovala/ jsem.
[ʒertoval /ʒertovala/ jsɛm]

Are you serious?
Myslíte to vážně?
[mɪsliːtɛ to vaːʒne?]

I'm serious.
Myslím to vážně.
[mɪsliːm to vaːʒne]

Really?!
Opravdu?!
[opravdu?!]

It's unbelievable!
To je neuvěřitelné!
[to jɛ nɛuverʒɪtɛlnɛː!]

I don't believe you.
Nevěřím vám.
[nɛverʒiːm vaːm]

I can't.
Nemůžu.
[nɛmuːʒu]

I don't know.
Nevím.
[nɛviːm]

I don't understand you.
Nerozumím vám.
[nɛrozumiːm vaːm]

Please go away. | **Odejděte prosím.**
[odɛjdetɛ prosi:m]

Leave me alone! | **Nechte mě na pokoji!**
[nɛxtɛ mne na pokojɪ!]

I can't stand him. | **Nesnáším ho.**
[nɛsna:ʃi:m ho]

You are disgusting! | **Jste odporný!**
[jstɛ otporni:!]

I'll call the police! | **Zavolám policii!**
[zavola:m polɪtsɪjɪ!]

Sharing impressions. Emotions

I like it.	**Líbí se mi to.** [li:bi: sɛ mɪ to]
Very nice.	**Moc pěkné.** [mots pɛknɛ:]
That's great!	**To je skvělé!** [to jɛ skvelɛ:!]
It's not bad.	**To není špatné.** [to nɛni: ʃpatnɛ:]

I don't like it.	**Nelíbí se mi to.** [nɛli:bi: sɛ mɪ to]
It's not good.	**To není dobře.** [to nɛni: dobrʒɛ]
It's bad.	**To je špatné.** [to jɛ ʃpatnɛ:]
It's very bad.	**Je to moc špatné.** [jɛ to mots ʃpatnɛ:]
It's disgusting.	**To je odporné.** [to jɛ otpornɛ:]

I'm happy.	**Jsem šťastný /šťastná/.** [jsɛm ʃtʲastni: /ʃtʲastna:/]
I'm content.	**Jsem spokojený /spokojená/.** [jsɛm spokojɛni: /spokojɛna:/]
I'm in love.	**Jsem zamilovaný /zamilovaná/.** [jsɛm zamɪlovani: /zamɪlovana:/]
I'm calm.	**Jsem klidný /klidná/.** [jsɛm klɪdni: /klɪdna:/]
I'm bored.	**Nudím se.** [nudi:m sɛ]

I'm tired.	**Jsem unavený /unavená/.** [jsɛm unavɛni: /unavɛna:/]
I'm sad.	**Jsem smutný /smutná/.** [jsɛm smutni: /smutna:/]
I'm frightened.	**Jsem vystrašený /vystrašená/.** [jsɛm vɪstraʃɛni: /vɪstraʃɛna:/]

I'm angry.	**Zlobím se.** [zlobi:m sɛ]
I'm worried.	**Mám starosti.** [ma:m starostɪ]
I'm nervous.	**Jsem nervózní.** [jsɛm nɛrvózni:]

I'm jealous. (envious) **Žárlím.**
[ʒaːrliːm]

I'm surprised. **Jsem překvapený /překvapená/.**
[jsɛm prʒɛkvapɛni: /prʒɛkvapɛna:/]

I'm perplexed. **Jsem zmatený /zmatená/.**
[jsɛm zmatɛni: /zmatɛna:/]

Problems. Accidents

I've got a problem.

Mám problém.
[ma:m problɛ:m]

We've got a problem.

Máme problém.
[ma:mɛ problɛ:m]

I'm lost.

Ztratil /Ztratila/ jsem se.
[stratɪl /stratɪla/ jsɛm sɛ]

I missed the last bus (train).

Zmeškal /Zmeškala/ jsem poslední autobus (vlak).
[zmɛʃkal /zmɛʃkala/ jsɛm poslɛdni: autobus (vlak)]

I don't have any money left.

Už nemám žádné peníze.
[uʒ nɛma:m ʒa:dnɛ: pɛni:zɛ]

I've lost my ...

Ztratil /Ztratila/ jsem ...
[stratɪl /stratɪla/ jsɛm ...]

Someone stole my ...

Někdo mi ukradl ...
[nɛgdo mɪ ukradl ...]

passport

pas
[pas]

wallet

peněženku
[pɛneʒɛŋku]

papers

dokumenty
[dokumɛntɪ]

ticket

vstupenku
[vstupɛŋku]

money

peníze
[pɛni:zɛ]

handbag

kabelku
[kabɛlku]

camera

fotoaparát
[fotoapara:t]

laptop

počítač
[potʃi:tatʃ]

tablet computer

tablet
[tablɛt]

mobile phone

mobilní telefon
[mobɪlni: tɛlɛfon]

Help me!

Pomozte mi!
[pomoztɛ mɪ!]

What's happened?

Co se stalo?
[tso sɛ stalo?]

fire	**požár** [poʒaːr]
shooting	**střelba** [strʒɛlba]
murder	**vražda** [vraʒda]
explosion	**výbuch** [viːbux]
fight	**rvačka** [rvatʃka]

Call the police!	**Zavolejte policii!** [zavolɛjtɛ polɪtsɪjɪ!]
Please hurry up!	**Pospěšte si prosím!** [pospeʃtɛ sɪ prosiːm!]
I'm looking for the police station.	**Hledám policejní stanici.** [hlɛdaːm polɪtsɛjniː stanɪtsɪ]
I need to make a call.	**Potřebuju si zavolat.** [potrʒɛbuju sɪ zavolat]
May I use your phone?	**Můžu si od vás zavolat?** [muːʒu sɪ od vaːs zavolat?]

I've been …	**Byl /Byla/ jsem …** [bɪl /bɪla/ jsɛm …]
mugged	**přepaden /přepadena/** [prʃɛpadɛn /prʃɛpadɛna/]
robbed	**oloupen /oloupena/** [oloupɛn /oloupɛna/]
raped	**znásilněna** [znaːsɪlnena]
attacked (beaten up)	**napaden /napadena/** [napadɛn /napadɛna/]

Are you all right?	**Jste v pořádku?** [jstɛ v porʒaːtku?]
Did you see who it was?	**Viděl /Viděla/ jste, kdo to byl?** [vɪdel /vɪdela/ jstɛ, gdo to bɪl?]
Would you be able to recognize the person?	**Poznal /Poznala/ byste toho člověka?** [poznal /poznala/ bɪstɛ toho tʃloveka?]
Are you sure?	**Jste si tím jist /jista/?** [jstɛ sɪ tiːm jɪst /jɪsta/?]

Please calm down.	**Uklidněte se, prosím.** [uklɪdnetɛ sɛ, prosiːm]
Take it easy!	**Uklidněte se!** [uklɪdnetɛ sɛ!]
Don't worry!	**Nebojte se!** [nɛbojtɛ sɛ!]
Everything will be fine.	**Všechno bude v pořádku.** [vʃɛxno budɛ v porʒaːtku]
Everything's all right.	**Vše v pořádku.** [vʃɛ v porʒaːtku]

Come here, please.

Pojďte sem, prosím.
[pojdⁱtɛ sɛm, prosi:m]

I have some questions for you.

Mám na vás několik otázek.
[ma:m na va:s nekolɪk ota:zɛk]

Wait a moment, please.

Okamžik, prosím.
[okamʒɪk, prosi:m]

Do you have any I.D.?

Máte nějaký průkaz totožnosti?
[ma:tɛ nejaki: pru:kaz totoʒnostɪ?]

Thanks. You can leave now.

Díky. Teď můžete odejít.
[di:kɪ. tɛdʲ mu:ʒetɛ odɛji:t]

Hands behind your head!

Ruce za hlavu!
[rutsɛ za hlavu!]

You're under arrest!

Jste zatčen /zatčena/!
[jstɛ zattʃɛn /zattʃɛna/!]

Health problems

Please help me.	**Prosím vás, pomozte mi.** [prosi:m va:s, pomoztɛ mɪ]
I don't feel well.	**Necítím se dobře.** [nɛtsi:ti:m sɛ dobrʒɛ]
My husband doesn't feel well.	**Můj manžel se necítí dobře.** [mu:j manʒel sɛ nɛtsi:ti: dobrʒe]
My son …	**Můj syn …** [mu:j sɪn …]
My father …	**Můj otec …** [mu:j otɛts …]

My wife doesn't feel well.	**Moje manželka se necítí dobře.** [mojɛ manʒelka sɛ nɛtsi:ti: dobrʒe]
My daughter …	**Moje dcera …** [mojɛ dtsɛra …]
My mother …	**Moje matka …** [mojɛ matka …]

I've got a …	**Bolí mě …** [boli: mne …]
headache	**hlava** [hlava]
sore throat	**v krku** [v krku]
stomach ache	**žaludek** [ʒaludɛk]
toothache	**zub** [zup]

I feel dizzy.	**Mám závratě.** [ma:m za:vrate]
He has a fever.	**On má horečku.** [on ma: horɛtʃku]
She has a fever.	**Ona má horečku.** [ona ma: horɛtʃku]
I can't breathe.	**Nemůžu dýchat.** [nɛmu:ʒu di:xat]

I'm short of breath.	**Nemůžu se nadechnout.** [nɛmu:ʒu sɛ nadɛxnout]
I am asthmatic.	**Jsem astmatik /astmatička/.** [jsɛm astmatɪk /astmatɪtʃka/]
I am diabetic.	**Jsem diabetik /diabetička/.** [jsɛm dɪabɛtɪk /dɪabɛtɪtʃka/]

I can't sleep.	**Nemůžu spát.** [nɛmuːʒu spaːt]
food poisoning	**otrava z jídla** [otrava z jiːdla]

It hurts here.	**Tady to bolí.** [tadɪ to boliː]
Help me!	**Pomozte mi!** [pomoztɛ mɪ!]
I am here!	**Tady jsem!** [tadɪ jsɛm!]
We are here!	**Tady jsme!** [tadɪ jsmɛ!]
Get me out of here!	**Dostaňte mě odtud!** [dostanˈtɛ mne odtut!]
I need a doctor.	**Potřebuju doktora.** [potrʒɛbuju doktora]
I can't move.	**Nemůžu se hýbat.** [nɛmuːʒu sɛ hiːbat]
I can't move my legs.	**Nemůžu hýbat nohama.** [nɛmuːʒu hiːbat nohama]

I have a wound.	**Jsem zraněný /zraněná/.** [jsɛm zraneniː /zranenaː/]
Is it serious?	**Je to vážné?** [jɛ to vaːʒnɛ:?]
My documents are in my pocket.	**Doklady mám v kapse.** [dokladɪ maːm v kapsɛ]
Calm down!	**Uklidněte se!** [uklɪdnetɛ sɛ!]
May I use your phone?	**Můžu si od vás zavolat?** [muːʒu sɪ od vaːs zavolat?]

Call an ambulance!	**Zavolejte sanitku!** [zavolɛjtɛ sanɪtku!]
It's urgent!	**Je to urgentní!** [jɛ to urgɛntniː!]
It's an emergency!	**To je pohotovost!** [to jɛ pohotovost!]
Please hurry up!	**Prosím vás, pospěšte si!** [prosiːm vaːs, pospeʃtɛ sɪ!]
Would you please call a doctor?	**Zavolal /Zavolala/ byste prosím lékaře?** [zavolal /zavolala/ bɪstɛ prosiːm lɛːkarʒɛ?]
Where is the hospital?	**Kde je nemocnice?** [gdɛ jɛ nɛmotsnɪtsɛ?]

How are you feeling?	**Jak se cítíte?** [jak sɛ tsiːtiːtɛ?]
Are you all right?	**Jste v pořádku?** [jstɛ v porʒaːtku?]

What's happened?	**Co se stalo?** [tso sɛ stalo?]
I feel better now.	**Teď už se cítím líp.** [tɛdʲ uʒ sɛ tsi:ti:m li:p]
It's OK.	**To je v pořádku.** [to jɛ v porʒa:tku]
It's all right.	**To je v pořádku.** [to jɛ v porʒa:tku]

At the pharmacy

pharmacy (drugstore)

lékárna
[lɛːkaːrna]

24-hour pharmacy

non-stop lékárna
[non-stop lɛːkaːrna]

Where is the closest pharmacy?

Kde je nejbližší lékárna?
[gdɛ jɛ nɛjblɪʒʃiː leːkaːrna?]

Is it open now?

Mají teď otevřeno?
[majiː tɛdʲ otɛvrʒɛno?]

At what time does it open?

V kolik hodin otvírají?
[v kolɪk hodɪn otviːrajiː?]

At what time does it close?

V kolik hodin zavírají?
[v kolɪk hodɪn zaviːrajiː?]

Is it far?

Je to daleko?
[jɛ to dalɛko?]

Can I get there on foot?

Dostanu se tam pěšky?
[dostanu sɛ tam pɛʃkɪ?]

Can you show me on the map?

Můžete mi to ukázat na mapě?
[muːʒetɛ mɪ to ukaːzat na mape?]

Please give me something for ...

Můžete mi prosím vás dát něco na ...
[muːʒetɛ mɪ prosiːm vaːs daːt netso na]

a headache

bolení hlavy
[bolɛniː hlavɪ]

a cough

kašel
[kaʃɛl]

a cold

nachlazení
[naxlazɛniː]

the flu

chřipka
[xrʃɪpka]

a fever

horečka
[horɛtʃka]

a stomach ache

bolesti v žaludku
[bolɛstɪ v ʒalutku]

nausea

nucení na zvracení
[nutsɛniː na zvratsɛniː]

diarrhea

průjem
[pruːjɛm]

constipation

zácpa
[zaːtspa]

pain in the back	**bolest v zádech** [bolɛst v za:dɛx]
chest pain	**bolest na hrudi** [bolɛst na hrudɪ]
side stitch	**boční steh** [botʃni: stɛh]
abdominal pain	**bolest břicha** [bolɛst brʒɪxa]

pill	**pilulka** [pɪlulka]
ointment, cream	**mast, krém** [mast, krɛ:m]
syrup	**sirup** [sɪrup]
spray	**sprej** [sprɛj]
drops	**kapky** [kapkɪ]

You need to go to the hospital.	**Musíte jít do nemocnice.** [musi:tɛ ji:t do nɛmotsnɪtsɛ]
health insurance	**zdravotní pojištění** [zdravotni: pojɪʃteni:]
prescription	**předpis** [prʃɛtpɪs]
insect repellant	**repelent proti hmyzu** [rɛpɛlɛnt protɪ hmɪzu]
Band Aid	**náplast** [na:plast]

The bare minimum

Excuse me, ...	**Promiňte, ...** [promɪnʲtɛ, ...]
Hello.	**Dobrý den.** [dobriː dɛn]
Thank you.	**Děkuji.** [dekujɪ]
Good bye.	**Na shledanou.** [na sxlɛdanou]
Yes.	**Ano.** [ano]
No.	**Ne.** [nɛ]
I don't know.	**Nevím.** [nɛviːm]
Where? | Where to? | When?	**Kde? | Kam? | Kdy?** [gdɛ? | kam? | gdɪ?]
I need ...	**Potřebuju ...** [potrʒɛbuju ...]
I want ...	**Chci ...** [xtsɪ ...]
Do you have ...?	**Máte ...?** [maːtɛ ...?]
Is there a ... here?	**Je tady ...?** [jɛ tadɪ ...?]
May I ...?	**Můžu ...?** [muːʒu ...?]
..., please (polite request)	**..., prosím** [..., prosiːm]
I'm looking for ...	**Hledám ...** [hlɛdaːm ...]
the restroom	**toaletu** [toalɛtu]
an ATM	**bankomat** [baŋkomat]
a pharmacy (drugstore)	**lékárnu** [lɛːkaːrnu]
a hospital	**nemocnici** [nɛmotsnɪtsɪ]
the police station	**policejní stanici** [polɪtsɛjniː stanɪtsɪ]
the subway	**metro** [mɛtro]

a taxi	**taxík** [taksi:k]
the train station	**vlakové nádraží** [vlakovɛ: na:draʒi:]

My name is …	**Jmenuju se …** [jmɛnuju sɛ …]
What's your name?	**Jak se jmenujete?** [jak sɛ jmɛnujɛtɛ?]
Could you please help me?	**Můžete mi prosím pomoct?** [mu:ʒetɛ mɪ prosi:m pomotst?]
I've got a problem.	**Mám problém.** [ma:m problɛ:m]
I don't feel well.	**Necítím se dobře.** [nɛtsi:ti:m sɛ dobrʒɛ]
Call an ambulance!	**Zavolejte sanitku!** [zavolɛjtɛ sanɪtku!]
May I make a call?	**Můžu si zavolat?** [mu:ʒu sɪ zavolat?]

I'm sorry.	**Omlouvám se.** [omlouva:m sɛ]
You're welcome.	**Není zač.** [nɛni: zatʃ]

I, me	**Já** [ja:]
you (inform.)	**ty** [tɪ]
he	**on** [on]
she	**ona** [ona]
they (masc.)	**oni** [onɪ]
they (fem.)	**ony** [onɪ]
we	**my** [mɪ]
you (pl)	**vy** [vɪ]
you (sg, form.)	**vy** [vɪ]

ENTRANCE	**VCHOD** [vxot]
EXIT	**VÝCHOD** [vi:xot]
OUT OF ORDER	**MIMO PROVOZ** [mɪmo provos]
CLOSED	**ZAVŘENO** [zavrʒɛno]

OPEN	**OTEVŘENO**
	[otɛvrʒɛno]
FOR WOMEN	**ŽENY**
	[ʒenɪ]
FOR MEN	**MUŽI**
	[muʒɪ]

MINI DICTIONARY

This section contains 250 useful words required for everyday communication. You will find the names of months and days of the week here. The dictionary also contains topics such as colors, measurements, family, and more

T&P Books Publishing

DICTIONARY CONTENTS

T&P Books Publishing

1. Time. Calendar

time	**čas** (m)	[ʧas]
hour	**hodina** (ž)	[hodɪna]
half an hour	**půlhodina** (ž)	[pu:lhodɪna]
minute	**minuta** (ž)	[mɪnuta]
second	**sekunda** (ž)	[sɛkunda]
today (adv)	**dnes**	[dnɛs]
tomorrow (adv)	**zítra**	[zi:tra]
yesterday (adv)	**včera**	[vʧɛra]
Monday	**pondělí** (s)	[pondeli:]
Tuesday	**úterý** (s)	[u:tɛri:]
Wednesday	**středa** (ž)	[strʃɛda]
Thursday	**čtvrtek** (m)	[ʧtvrtɛk]
Friday	**pátek** (m)	[pa:tɛk]
Saturday	**sobota** (ž)	[sobota]
Sunday	**neděle** (ž)	[nɛdelɛ]
day	**den** (m)	[dɛn]
working day	**pracovní den** (m)	[praʦovni: dɛn]
public holiday	**sváteční den** (m)	[sva:tɛʧni: dɛn]
weekend	**víkend** (m)	[vi:kɛnt]
week	**týden** (m)	[ti:dɛn]
last week (adv)	**minulý týden**	[mɪnuli: ti:dɛn]
next week (adv)	**příští týden**	[prʃi:ʃti: ti:dɛn]
in the morning	**ráno**	[ra:no]
in the afternoon	**odpoledne**	[otpolɛdnɛ]
in the evening	**večer**	[vɛʧɛr]
tonight (this evening)	**dnes večer**	[dnɛs vɛʧɛr]
at night	**v noci**	[v noʦɪ]
midnight	**půlnoc** (ž)	[pu:lnoʦ]
January	**leden** (m)	[lɛdɛn]
February	**únor** (m)	[u:nor]
March	**březen** (m)	[brʒɛzɛn]
April	**duben** (m)	[dubɛn]
May	**květen** (m)	[kvetɛn]
June	**červen** (m)	[ʧɛrvɛn]
July	**červenec** (m)	[ʧɛrvɛnɛʦ]
August	**srpen** (m)	[srpɛn]

September	září (s)	[zaːrʒiː]
October	říjen (m)	[rʒiːjɛn]
November	listopad (m)	[lɪstopat]
December	prosinec (m)	[prosɪnɛʦ]

in spring	na jaře	[na jarʒɛ]
in summer	v létě	[v lɛːte]
in fall	na podzim	[na podzɪm]
in winter	v zimě	[v zɪmne]

month	měsíc (m)	[mnesiːʦ]
season (summer, etc.)	období (s)	[obdobiː]
year	rok (m)	[rok]

2. Numbers. Numerals

0 zero	nula (ż)	[nula]
1 one	jeden	[jɛdɛn]
2 two	dva	[dva]
3 three	tři	[trʃɪ]
4 four	čtyři	[ʧtɪrʒɪ]

5 five	pět	[pet]
6 six	šest	[ʃɛst]
7 seven	sedm	[sɛdm]
8 eight	osm	[osm]
9 nine	devět	[dɛvet]
10 ten	deset	[dɛsɛt]

11 eleven	jedenáct	[jɛdɛnaːʦt]
12 twelve	dvanáct	[dvanaːʦt]
13 thirteen	třináct	[trʃɪnaːʦt]
14 fourteen	čtrnáct	[ʧtrnaːʦt]
15 fifteen	patnáct	[patnaːʦt]

16 sixteen	šestnáct	[ʃɛstnaːʦt]
17 seventeen	sedmnáct	[sɛdmnaːʦt]
18 eighteen	osmnáct	[osmnaːʦt]
19 nineteen	devatenáct	[dɛvatɛnaːʦt]

20 twenty	dvacet	[dvaʦɛt]
30 thirty	třicet	[trʃɪʦɛt]
40 forty	čtyřicet	[ʧtɪrʒɪʦɛt]
50 fifty	padesát	[padesaːt

60 sixty	šedesát	[ʃɛdɛsaːt
70 seventy	sedmdesát	[sɛdmdɛsaːt
80 eighty	osmdesát	[osmdɛsaːt
90 ninety	devadesát	[dɛvadɛsaːt
100 one hundred	sto	[sto]

200 two hundred	dvě stě	[dve ste]
300 three hundred	tři sta	[trʃɪ sta]
400 four hundred	čtyři sta	[tʃtɪrʒɪ sta]
500 five hundred	pět set	[pet sɛt]

600 six hundred	šest set	[ʃɛst sɛt]
700 seven hundred	sedm set	[sɛdm sɛt]
800 eight hundred	osm set	[osm sɛt]
900 nine hundred	devět set	[dɛvet sɛt]
1000 one thousand	tisíc (m)	[tɪsi:ts]

| 10000 ten thousand | deset tisíc | [dɛsɛt tɪsi:ts] |
| one hundred thousand | sto tisíc | [sto tɪsi:ts] |

| million | milión (m) | [mɪlɪo:n] |
| billion | miliarda (ž) | [mɪlɪarda] |

3. Humans. Family

man (adult male)	muž (m)	[muʃ]
young man	jinoch (m)	[jɪnox]
woman	žena (ž)	[ʒena]
girl (young woman)	slečna (ž)	[slɛtʃna]
old man	stařec (m)	[starʒɛts]
old woman	stařena (ž)	[starʒɛna]

mother	matka (ž)	[matka]
father	otec (m)	[otɛts]
son	syn (m)	[sɪn]
daughter	dcera (ž)	[dtsɛra]
brother	bratr (m)	[bratr]
sister	sestra (ž)	[sɛstra]

parents	rodiče (m mn)	[rodɪtʃɛ]
child	dítě (s)	[di:te]
children	děti (ž mn)	[detɪ]
stepmother	nevlastní matka (ž)	[nɛvlastni: matka]
stepfather	nevlastní otec (m)	[nɛvlastni: otɛts]

grandmother	babička (ž)	[babɪtʃka]
grandfather	dědeček (m)	[dedɛtʃɛk]
grandson	vnuk (m)	[vnuk]
granddaughter	vnučka (ž)	[vnutʃka]
grandchildren	vnuci (m mn)	[vnutsɪ]

uncle	strýc (m)	[stri:ts]
aunt	teta (ž)	[tɛta]
nephew	synovec (m)	[sɪnovɛts]
niece	neteř (ž)	[nɛtɛrʃ]
wife	žena (ž)	[ʒena]

husband	**muž** (m)	[muʃ]
married (masc.)	**ženatý**	[ʒenati:]
married (fem.)	**vdaná**	[vdana:]
widow	**vdova** (ž)	[vdova]
widower	**vdovec** (m)	[vdovɛʦ]
name (first name)	**jméno** (s)	[jmɛ:no]
surname (last name)	**příjmení** (s)	[prʃi:jmɛni:]
relative	**příbuzný** (m)	[prʃi:buzni:]
friend (masc.)	**přítel** (m)	[prʃi:tɛl]
friendship	**přátelství** (s)	[prʃa:tɛlstvi:]
partner	**partner** (m)	[partnɛr]
superior (n)	**vedoucí** (m)	[vɛdouʦi:]
colleague	**kolega** (m)	[kolɛga]
neighbors	**sousedé** (m mn)	[sousɛdɛ:]

4. Human body

body	**tělo** (s)	[telo]
heart	**srdce** (s)	[srdʦɛ]
blood	**krev** (ž)	[krɛf]
brain	**mozek** (m)	[mozɛk]
bone	**kost** (ž)	[kost]
spine (backbone)	**páteř** (ž)	[pa:tɛrʃ]
rib	**žebro** (s)	[ʒebro]
lungs	**plíce** (ž mn)	[pli:ʦɛ]
skin	**pleť** (ž)	[plɛtʲ]
head	**hlava** (ž)	[hlava]
face	**obličej** (ž)	[oblɪtʃɛj]
nose	**nos** (m)	[nos]
forehead	**čelo** (s)	[tʃɛlo]
cheek	**tvář** (ž)	[tva:rʃ]
mouth	**ústa** (s mn)	[u:sta]
tongue	**jazyk** (m)	[jazɪk]
tooth	**zub** (m)	[zup]
lips	**rty** (m mn)	[rtɪ]
chin	**brada** (ž)	[brada]
ear	**ucho** (s)	[uxo]
neck	**krk** (m)	[krk]
eye	**oko** (s)	[oko]
pupil	**zornice** (ž)	[zornɪʦɛ]
eyebrow	**obočí** (s)	[obotʃi:]
eyelash	**řasa** (ž)	[rʒasa]
hair	**vlasy** (m mn)	[vlasɪ]

hairstyle	účes (m)	[uːtʃɛs]
mustache	vousy (m mn)	[vousɪ]
beard	plnovous (m)	[plnovous]
to have (a beard, etc.)	nosit	[nosɪt]
bald (adj)	lysý	[lɪsiː]

hand	ruka (ž)	[ruka]
arm	ruka (ž)	[ruka]
finger	prst (m)	[prst]
nail	nehet (m)	[nɛhɛt]
palm	dlaň (ž)	[dlanʲ]

shoulder	rameno (s)	[ramɛno]
leg	noha (ž)	[noha]
knee	koleno (s)	[kolɛno]
heel	pata (ž)	[pata]
back	záda (s mn)	[zaːda]

5. Clothing. Personal accessories

clothes	oblečení (s)	[oblɛtʃɛniː]
coat (overcoat)	kabát (m)	[kabaːt]
fur coat	kožich (m)	[koʒɪx]
jacket (e.g., leather ~)	bunda (ž)	[bunda]
raincoat (trenchcoat, etc.)	plášť (m)	[plaːʃtʲ]

shirt (button shirt)	košile (ž)	[koʃɪlɛ]
pants	kalhoty (ž mn)	[kalhotɪ]
suit jacket	sako (s)	[sako]
suit	pánský oblek (m)	[paːnski: oblɛk]

dress (frock)	šaty (m mn)	[ʃatɪ]
skirt	sukně (ž)	[suknɛ]
T-shirt	tričko (s)	[trɪtʃko]
bathrobe	župan (m)	[ʒupan]
pajamas	pyžamo (s)	[pɪʒamo]
workwear	pracovní oděv (m)	[pratsovni: odef]

underwear	spodní prádlo (s)	[spodni: praːdlo]
socks	ponožky (ž mn)	[ponoʃkɪ]
bra	podprsenka (ž)	[potprsɛŋka]
pantyhose	punčochové kalhoty (ž mn)	[puntʃoxovɛ: kalgotɪ]
stockings (thigh highs)	punčochy (ž mn)	[puntʃoxɪ]
bathing suit	plavky (ž mn)	[plafkɪ]

hat	čepice (ž)	[tʃɛpɪtsɛ]
footwear	obuv (ž)	[obuf]
boots (e.g., cowboy ~)	holínky (ž mn)	[holiːŋkɪ]
heel	podpatek (m)	[potpatɛk]
shoestring	tkanička (ž)	[tkanɪtʃka]

shoe polish	krém (m) na boty	[krɛ:m na botɪ]
gloves	rukavice (ž mn)	[rukavɪʦɛ]
mittens	palčáky (m mn)	[palʧa:kɪ]
scarf (muffler)	šála (ž)	[ʃa:la]
glasses (eyeglasses)	brýle (ž mn)	[bri:lɛ]
umbrella	deštník (m)	[dɛʃtni:k]
tie (necktie)	kravata (ž)	[kravata]
handkerchief	kapesník (m)	[kapesni:k]
comb	hřeben (m)	[hrʒɛbɛn]
hairbrush	kartáč (m) na vlasy	[karta:ʧ na vlasɪ]
buckle	spona (ž)	[spona]
belt	pás (m)	[pa:s]
purse	kabelka (ž)	[kabɛlka]

6. House. Apartment

apartment	byt (m)	[bɪt]
room	pokoj (m)	[pokoj]
bedroom	ložnice (ž)	[loʒnɪʦɛ]
dining room	jídelna (ž)	[ji:dɛlna]
living room	přijímací pokoj (m)	[prʃɪji:maʦi: pokoj]
study (home office)	pracovna (ž)	[praʦovna]
entry room	předsíň (ž)	[prʃɛtsi:nʲ]
bathroom (room with a bath or shower)	koupelna (ž)	[koupɛlna]
half bath	záchod (m)	[za:xot]
vacuum cleaner	vysavač (m)	[vɪsavaʧ]
mop	mop (m)	[mop]
dust cloth	hadr (m)	[hadr]
short broom	koště (s)	[koʃtɛ]
dustpan	lopatka (ž) na smetí	[lopatka na smɛti:]
furniture	nábytek (m)	[na:bɪtɛk]
table	stůl (m)	[stu:l]
chair	židle (ž)	[ʒɪdlɛ]
armchair	křeslo (s)	[krʃɛslo]
mirror	zrcadlo (s)	[zrʦadlo]
carpet	koberec (m)	[kobɛrɛʦ]
fireplace	krb (m)	[krp]
drapes	záclony (ž mn)	[za:ʦlonɪ]
table lamp	stolní lampa (ž)	[stolni: lampa]
chandelier	lustr (m)	[lustr]
kitchen	kuchyně (ž)	[kuxɪne]
gas stove (range)	plynový sporák (m)	[plɪnovi: spora:k]

| electric stove | elektrický sporák (m) | [ɛlɛktrɪtski: spora:k] |
| microwave oven | mikrovlnná pec (ž) | [mɪkrovlnna: pɛts] |

refrigerator	lednička (ž)	[lɛdnɪtʃka]
freezer	mrazicí komora (ž)	[mrazɪtsi: komora]
dishwasher	myčka (ž) nádobí	[mɪtʃka na:dobi:]
faucet	kohout (m)	[kohout]

meat grinder	mlýnek (m) na maso	[mli:nɛk na maso]
juicer	odšťavňovač (m)	[otʃtʲavnʲovatʃ]
toaster	opékač (m) topinek	[opɛ:katʃ topɪnɛk]
mixer	mixér (m)	[mɪksɛ:r]

coffee machine	kávovar (m)	[ka:vovar]
kettle	čajník (m)	[tʃajni:k]
teapot	čajová konvice (ž)	[tʃajova: konvɪtsɛ]

TV set	televizor (m)	[tɛlɛvɪzor]
VCR (video recorder)	videomagnetofon (m)	[vɪdɛomagnɛtofon]
iron (e.g., steam ~)	žehlička (ž)	[ʒehlɪtʃka]
telephone	telefon (m)	[tɛlɛfon]

www.ingramcontent.com/pod-product-compliance
Lightning Source LLC
Chambersburg PA
CBHW070842050426

42452CB00011B/2384